JUNIOR PET CARE

BUDGERIGARS

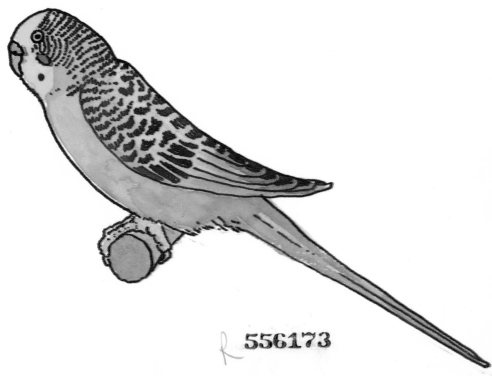

ZUZA VRBOVA

132 2890

Photography Susan C. Miller
Hugh Nicholas
Illustration Robert McAulay
Reading and Child Psychology Consultant
Dr. David Lewis

ACKNOWLEDGMENTS

With special thanks to Jenny Toft at Pet Bowl; Barry and Kay Sayers; Maypole Pet & Garden Centre; Mr. Hollingsworth, Animal Breeder; Lesley and Rebecca Sharpe; Craig Dellow; Menor Photographic Services.

Library of Congress #89-52056

Distributed in the UNITED STATES by T.F.H. Publications, Inc., One T.F.H. Plaza, Neptune City, NJ 07753; in CANADA to the Pet Trade by H & L Pet Supplies Inc., 27 Kingston Crescent, Kitchener, Ontario N2B 2T6; Rolf C. Hagen Ltd., 3225 Sartelon Street, Montreal 382 Quebec; in CANADA to the Book Trade by Macmillan of Canada (A Division of Canada Publishing Corporation), 164 Commander Boulevard, Agincourt, Ontario M1S 3C7; in ENGLAND by T.F.H. Publications, The Spinney, Parklands, Portsmouth PO7 6AR; in AUSTRALIA AND THE SOUTH PACIFIC by T.F.H. (Australia) Pty. Ltd., Box 149, Brookvale 2100 N.S.W., Australia; in NEW ZEALAND by Ross Haines & Son, Ltd., 82 D Elizabeth Knox Place, Panmure, Auckland, New Zealand; in the PHILIPPINES by Bio-Research, 5 Lippay Street, San Lorenzo Village, Makati Rizal; in SOUTH AFRICA by Multipet Pty. Ltd., Box 235 New Germany, South Africa 3620. Published by T.F.H. Publications, Inc. Manufactured in the United States of America by T.F.H. Publications, Inc.

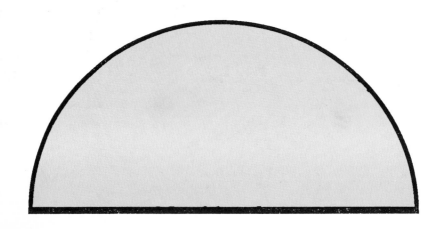

CONTENTS

NOTE TO PARENTS

Children are fascinated by birds, but most of the birds they come across are shy and fly away. Budgies are different. They like to perch on a child's finger and they can talk. ***BUDGIES*** shows children how to appreciate their beautiful, flying, friendly pet. The book has been specially written for children age 7 years and upwards and will inspire any child to develop the patience to bring up and care for a cheerful bird companion.

You and Your Budgie

A budgerigar (buj-er-ee-gar) is a beautiful bird and easy to take care of. If you look after your budgie, it will probably stay fit and healthy all its life—for seven or eight years. Many people call budgerigars parakeets.

The more time you spend with your budgie—talking to it and playing with it—the more friendly and tame it will become.

A budgie that is loved and well cared for will soon become part of the family and a special and lively companion for you.

Talking and taming

Probably the most exciting and challenging part of owning a budgie is teaching it how to talk. It is important to remember that each budgie is different and will learn at his own pace. A budgie may pick up talking very quickly, or only learn one or two words. But teaching your budgie to talk is a lot of fun. If you are serious about it you will eventually get results. If you have only one budgie, it

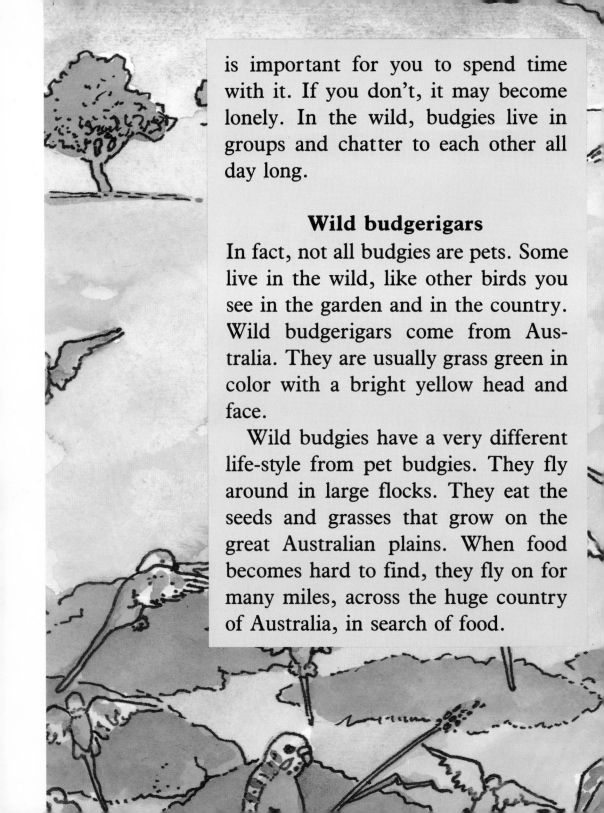

is important for you to spend time with it. If you don't, it may become lonely. In the wild, budgies live in groups and chatter to each other all day long.

Wild budgerigars

In fact, not all budgies are pets. Some live in the wild, like other birds you see in the garden and in the country. Wild budgerigars come from Australia. They are usually grass green in color with a bright yellow head and face.

Wild budgies have a very different life-style from pet budgies. They fly around in large flocks. They eat the seeds and grasses that grow on the great Australian plains. When food becomes hard to find, they fly on for many miles, across the huge country of Australia, in search of food.

2
CHOOSING A
BUDGIE

The best way to buy a budgie is to go to a pet store to choose one. You can buy one single budgie, two budgies, or if you have a large enough cage, several budgies.

One single budgie will not be lonely if you are prepared to give it lots of your time. But, if you are very busy and don't have much time to spend with your budgie or if you have to leave your pet sometimes, on the weekend for example, it is best to buy two budgies. Then they will be able to keep each other company while you are away.

A male budgie is called a **cock** and a female budgie is called a **hen.** If you do buy two budgies, it is most sensible to choose two cocks since hens tend to fight with each other.

Talking budgies

All budgies are able to learn to talk. But some budgies take a longer time than others to learn. When you are at the pet store choosing your budgie there is no way to tell whether a budgie will learn to talk easily or not. You will not be able to predict how many hours it will take to teach your budgie to talk. It is mainly luck whether you pick one that will easily become a good talker.

A spectacular budgie can be just one single color. You can buy a Lutino, which is a buttercup yellow, or an Albino which is pure white. Both these kinds have no other markings on their bodies.

The age of your budgie

When you go to the pet store to buy your budgie, ask to see those that are about six weeks old. A youngster of

this age will be easier for you to tame than a grown up one.

By six weeks of age a budgie would have left its nest and will be ready to go to a new home. A budgie that has recently left its nest may even be friendly enough to sit on your finger if you offer your finger as a perch in its cage.

The season to buy a budgie
Most baby budgies hatch out of an egg in the summer and early fall. Since you will be looking for a six– to eight–week–old budgie, you will probably find the largest choice available toward the end of the summer.

If you want to teach your budgie to talk, it is often better to buy one single budgie. Two budgies will chatter to each other.

13

Picking out a youngster

If you look carefully, you will be able to see the difference between a young budgie and a grown up budgie. Besides the overall appearance of a youngster with small fluffy feathers that make the budgie look babyish, there are some clear pointers.

First look at the eyes. A young budgie's eyes will be one solid, dark color while a budgie of more than twelve weeks of age will have a white ring around the central part of its eye.

Then look at the top of the budgie's head. A young budgie has a wavy pattern of feathers on the top of its head while a grown-up's forehead is one plain color.

Finally, you might also be able to tell if a budgie is a youngster by the "spots" on the neck area. They are long in shape in a young budgie, larger as the budgie grows.

A very young budgie—only a few days old—in its nesting box.

Male and female budgies

Naturally when you pick your budgie you will want to know whether it is a

A youngster being held. It is not old enough yet to go to a new home.

A comparison between a hen and a cock (below).

male or a female. In young budgies this can be hard to tell and you will have to look very carefully. When you look at budgies you will notice that they all have a colored fleshy area just above their beaks. This is the part of the budgie's body that is like a nose. It contains the nostrils and is called the **cere.**

Grown-up male budgies, cocks, have a blue cere and grown-up female budgies, hens, always have a brown cere. You can tell if the budgie is a cock or a hen by looking at the color of its cere.

But, in young budgies, the color difference of the cere is not so clear. Young cocks have a slightly more prominent and more purplish cere than hens.

A sky blue male cock perching in a comfortable aviary.

The colors of budgies

Budgies come in many different colors. Budgies are prized for their bright and unusual color combinations of green, blue, yellow and white. They are also solid colored.

It is fun to learn the names of new colors by looking at budgies. You can have budgies that come in different shades of green—light green, dark green or olive—that have bright yellow faces. Blue cobalt (a bright blue color) and rosy pink budgies have white faces.

Budgies come in all kinds of spectacular and brilliant colors.

Choosing the right budgie

When you go to the pet store to buy

your budgie, look at the available selection carefully. Although it is fun choosing the color you like best, it is most important for you to buy a healthy, happy budgie.

Watch the budgies in their cage at the pet store. Look for one that appears to be chirpy and lively and has bright eyes.

Taking your budgie home

Rather than bringing your budgie home in a cage, which might upset your new young pet, take it home in a small cardboard box. Pet stores usually provide specially made carrying boxes.

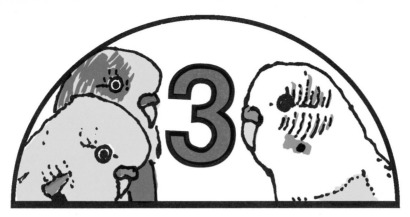

3

AN INDOOR HOME

You will see many different kinds of cages in the pet store. The cage that you buy should be as large as possible because the amount of exercise space your budgie has is important for its development and health.

If you plan to allow your budgie to fly around for most of the day, the cage does not need to be very large since it will only be used for resting at night time.

Comfort for your budgie

When you choose a place to put the cage try to think of where your budgie would be most comfortable. Budgies like to be in a spot with plenty of light and fresh air.

You can buy a metal stand to suspend the cage from. This is a good idea and makes the budgie the center of attention in the room.

A metal stand means you can move the cage around easily, to suit your budgie's needs. But, wherever the cage is, it must be in a safe place where it cannot be knocked over by accident.

Perches in the cage

Most cages come complete with perches for your budgie to rest on. If the perch is made of plastic you should exchange it for one made of natural wood since plastic perches are uncomfortable for budgies. Birds in cages with plastic perches often hold onto the sides of their cage rather than using their perch.

The best material for a perch is a tree branch. The wood from a sycamore or an apple tree is especially good. Branches vary in thickness so

A budgie clinging to the side of its cage because it has blisters on its feet from a plastic perch.

PROVIDING A WOODEN PERCH

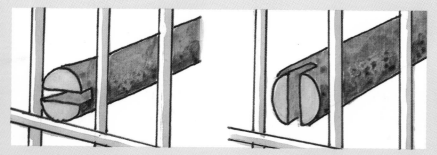

Cut a notch into a branch so that it fits snugly onto the bars of the cage. A grown-up should help you do this. Alternatively, you can re-use the tips normally fitted to plastic perches which slot into the bars of the cage.

that the budgie can vary its grip. Cut the branches so that they comfortably fit within the cage and avoid putting pressure on the bars.

Spacing the perches

Take care not to crowd the perches in one part of the cage as the budgie's tail may rub on one of them and cause its feathers to rip and tear.

You will probably only be able to fit two perches into your cage in order to make sure that they do not hang over seed and water containers.

Cage toys

Pet budgies enjoy playing with toys in their cage. But do not clutter the cage with toys. Too many toys may distract a young bird and prevent it from moving around freely in the cage.

Just like you, budgies often prefer the simplest and safest toys, like the Nylabird ring, for example. They can play with this and gnaw on it, which helps to keep their beak short.

Swings are often a part of the cage when you buy it. Your budgie may have great fun on a swing but if it does not use the swing at all, remove the swing. You can replace it with an extra, higher perch since budgies like to find the highest site to perch as darkness falls.

The Nylabird Dumbbell and Perch Ring

This perch ring and dumbbell are good for budgies to chew on. They are toys that have been specially designed for budgies. They contain calcium which helps to keep budgies healthy. Budgies like to chew things and it is better to provide them with safe and healthy toys like these than letting a budgie chew the bars and perches of its cage or other dangerous objects.

Budgies like mirrors. If you put a small mirror at the end of the perch, your budgie will probably spend hours talking to its own reflection.

Besides putting a perch in the cage, a ladder and a bell will also keep your budgie amused and will stop it from becoming bored.

The floor of the cage

Budgies like to have sand on the floor

of the cage. It gives them a chance to scratch and use their claws. You can either buy loose sand to line the floor of the cage or use a sand sheet. You can buy these from any pet store and they are ideal for the flooring in the cage. They make the cage easy to keep clean and are much less messy than loose sand.

Cleaning the cage is an important part of keeping a budgie. This job is much easier to do if you buy a cage with a removable base.

Avoid cages with clear plastic bases because a very young budgie might not realize that you can see through the plastic but not actually fly through it. It can become upset, running up and down the floor.

Bathing your budgie will be a special treat for it. Besides providing your budgie with a special bird bath, available at a local pet store, you can hang its cage outside during a warm shower of rain. If you do this, allow plenty of time for your budgie to get dry before night time, otherwise it might catch a cold.

Not all budgies like to be bathed and if your budgie avoids the bath, you can spray it using a plant sprayer, once or twice a week. This will keep your budgie's feathers in tip-top condition.

The water you shower your budgie with should be slightly warm—like the temperature of your own shower. Direct the spray so that the water

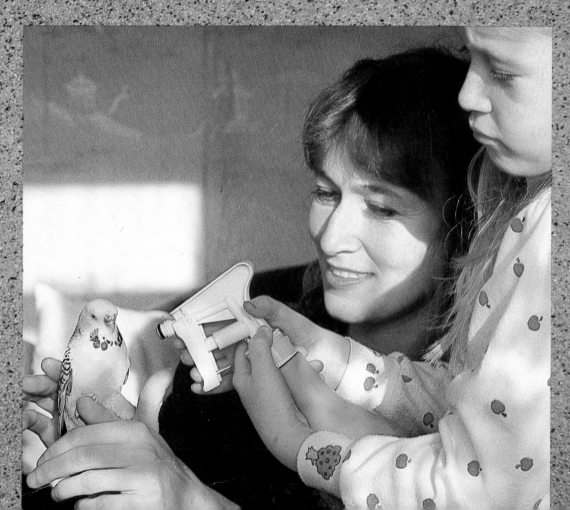

Pet budgies are very mischievous and interested in everything that is going on in the house, especially any bright objects.

falls from above, onto the budgie's head, like rain would do.

Remember to take the food and grit pots out of the cage before you give your budgie a shower. Your budgie may seem a little nervous about the shower at first but will probably become used to it and begin enjoying it.

Exercise for your budgie
A budgerigar needs exercise and will enjoy being let out of its cage to fly

around the room. There are some important things you must check for and do before you let your budgie out.

Make sure that all the doors and windows are firmly closed and that any open fires are protected by a screen as your budgie may be attracted by a fire.

Another possible danger is a deep vase filled with flowers. Budgies like water so much, your pet could try to take a bath in the vase but the water could be dangerously deep.

Happy and healthy, this budgie is enjoying its *Nylabird* perch with its owner.

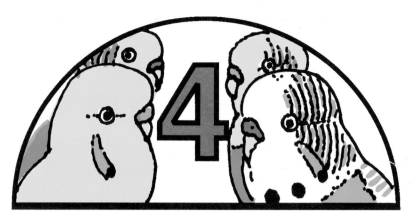

AN OUTDOOR HOME

Some people prefer to keep their budgies outdoors in an **aviary** all year round.

An aviary is usually divided into two parts. The outer section is made of a wooden frame and wire meshing. This is called the **flight** and should be big enough for birds to fly around comfortably in. Budgies do not mind being housed outdoors all year round but they do not like drafty or windy weather and they need some protection from the rain.

Budgies in an aviary.

The second part of the aviary is specially built to keep the budgies warm at night or when it gets cold. It is attached to the flight and is called the **shelter.** It looks like a garden shed.

If you do have an outdoor aviary, the flight area should not be full of too many swings or other obstacles. Try to provide as much free-flying flight space as possible.

Natural branches of hazel, willow, apple, pear or plum trees can be used to make perches in the flight area.

The advantage of natural wood

Remember to shut the outer door of the aviary when you take your budgies into their outdoor home.

perches is that budgies will be able to gnaw on them. This means that they chew on the wooden branch with their beaks—the kind of habit they have in the wild. It is very good for them because it prevents their beaks from becoming overgrown.

You can also hang a basket containing green food, which your budgies will enjoy, in the flight area.

If your budgie is hard to catch you can use a net in the aviary, as the man in the picture (above) is doing.

TRIMMING THE CLAWS

A grown-up or a veterinarian will probably need to clip your budgie's claws sometimes. This will help it to perch comfortably. The job is best done with special claw clippers.

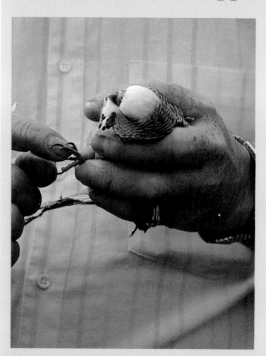 

HOLDING YOUR BUDGIE

With practice you will be able to hold your budgie comfortably and easily. You need to be firm but gentle. Use your hand to envelope the budgie's back but do not hold its neck too tightly otherwise it will not be able to breathe.

CLIPPING THE WINGS

If a budgie is very difficult to catch once it has been let out of the cage, some people decide to clip a wing. This is not dangerous for the budgie and does not hurt it.

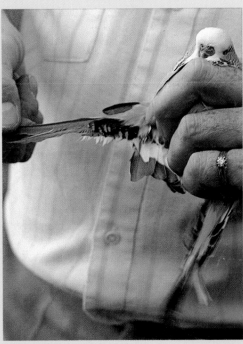

Never try to clip a wing yourself but ask a grown-up or a veterinarian for help. The budgie is held firmly in one hand and one wing is opened out. Several of the secondary flight feathers are cut off. Wing clipping may seem like a fierce and cruel thing to do but it is painless and temporary. The feathers that have been cut off do grow again.

FEEDING
YOUR BUDGIE

Wild budgerigars mainly eat the seed from different kinds of grasses. Your pet budgie will like similar kinds of seed and you can buy mixtures of bird seed, specially prepared for budgies, from most pet stores.

Besides simply eating bird seed, pet budgies need and enjoy having other kinds of food. The food that you feed your budgie should contain vitamins and minerals. These help to keep your budgie fit and healthy, just as they do in your own food.

Millet is a sure favorite with budgies. They eat this plant when it is very ripe. It comes in bundles that look like dried up bunches of grass. You can give these to your budgie as a special treat, in addition to regular bird seed. The spray of millet (shown on this page) will

probably be eaten up imme-
diately.

Besides seed and millet sprays, you should sometimes give your budgie some green food. This has valuable vitamins that are essential for budgies, just as they are for you.

Grit is also an important part of a budgie's needs. This sounds strange at first and you may wonder why your budgie needs to eat these tiny stones that seem to be so distasteful to us.

Budgies, like all other birds, have no teeth. Instead of grinding and chewing the seed in their mouths, it is broken into small pieces in their stomachs. In birds this is called a **gizzard.** The grit you give your budgie goes to the gizzard and helps to grind up bird seed into small particles there.

A spray of millet

Besides helping to grind up a budgie's food, grit also contains minerals that are good for a budgie. Providing grit is an important part of caring for your budgie. It is better to leave the grit for your budgie to nibble on in a pot in the cage rather than scattering it on the floor where it will become dirty.

YOUR BUDGIE'S WATER

All budgies need fresh, clean water every day. Rather than providing this in a pot, which your budgie might use to bathe in, use a tubular water container. This will keep the budgie's drinking water clean. Keep it filled so that your budgie can drink whenever it wants.

◄ Birdseed

Grit ▾

You can give small slices of carrot, apple or orange to your budgie. Experiment by offering a variety; you will soon find out which flavors your budgie prefers.

Treats for your budgie
Special budgie treats are available in pet stores. But do not give your budgie too many, otherwise it might become too fat. If your budgie has put on weight, give it plain birdseed to eat and no special treats. Let it fly around as much as possible.

Calcium is another important mineral that your budgie needs to keep its claws, beak and feathers in good condition. We need calcium in a similar way—to keep our nails and bones hard. Much of our calcium comes from milk. Budgies do not drink milk but instead they like chewing on **cuttlefish bone.**

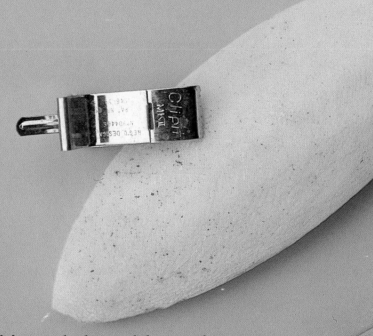

This oval-shaped bone does not look much like a bone at all but it is very rich in calcium. It can be fixed to the inside of the cage by a special clip.

An iodine nibble (right) fitted to the bars of the cage or the aviary mesh is also good for your budgie.

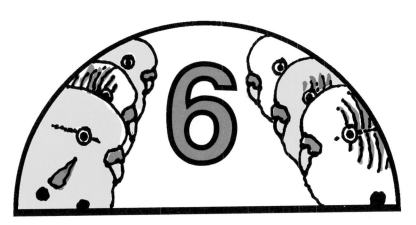

TAMING
YOUR BUDGIE

Budgies like to have company. It is easier to teach one budgie to talk because two budgies will talk to each other and distract each other in their own budgie language. Budgies like to chatter either to each other or to a person, so if you have one budgie it is important for you to spend plenty of time with it, otherwise it will become lonely.

Relaxing your budgie

At first, you will have to settle your young pet down in its new home and let it feel that it has nothing to fear.

The best way of doing this, besides making your budgie comfortable and feeding it correctly, is to spend as much time as possible with it. Before learning to talk, your budgie must learn not to be afraid of you.

As soon as your budgie seems to be relaxed in its new home you can try putting your hand gently into the cage. Put your finger out and encourage your budgie to use it as a perch. You might be able to coax it to sit on

**Make your
movements
slow but sure.**

your finger by touching the front of its legs gently. At this stage do not say anything. Just be very quiet.

Your budgie probably will not perch on your finger the first time you try putting your hand in the cage, but it might after a few days, once it is used to you.

Teaching your budgie to talk

When your budgie perches happily on your finger, you can start teaching it to talk. The first word you might like to teach your budgie is its name.

Hold the budgie on your finger, level with your face, and repeat its name and nothing else. You should do this regularly, several times a day until your budgie says its name back to you.

This may sound boring, but at first it is important not to confuse your budgie. You will be rewarded for repeating one word so patiently day after day when your budgie first tries to talk.

It is very exciting when your budgie starts to talk. All the hours you would have spent teaching it will seem completely worthwhile. Do not be surprised if your budgie cannot say its name very well at first. It will probably make strange throaty sounds, maybe for a few weeks until it can say its name.

It is a good idea to teach your budgie to say its name.

HEALTH CARE FOR YOUR BUDGIE

Budgerigars are usually healthy birds. But, if you feel that your budgie might be suffering from an illness, the best thing to do is to ask a grown-up to help you take it to a veterinarian as soon as possible.

The first symptoms of an illness are usually ruffled feathers and a dejected look with slow eyelid movement. This may be accompanied by heavy breathing and a jerky tail. If your budgie has been sick the feathers around its beak will be soiled and it soon loses its appetite.

If your bird is ill, the best and most useful thing to do is to provide plenty of warmth. Take your budgie to a warm part of the house and contact a veterinarian right away.

Stomach upsets

A budgie with an upset stomach becomes less active and its droppings may turn bright green. A stomach upset in budgerigars is often due to an infection.

If your budgie is suffering from these symptoms, take it to a veterinarian who will probably give it some medication. Be sure to follow the veterinarian's instructions on how much medication to give. Too much might worsen the situation and not taking enough medicine can cause problems too.

Sour crop

Sour crop is when part of the bird's body, called the crop, at the base of the neck is swollen with air.

Hens often suffer from this more than cocks. The most obvious symptom is some white discharge on the head of a bird that is suffering.

The quickest cure is to hold the budgerigar upside down and gently massage the neck area downwards. Ask a veterinarian for advice before you do this.

You can also add some purple crystals called potassium permanganate to the sick bird's drinking water. Your petstore owner will help you find what you're looking for. This makes the budgie's drinking water purple but should cure the budgie within two days.

Feather plucking

This is a bad habit when the bird nibbles its own feathers. The best thing to do is to provide toys to distract the budgie and spray it daily with warm water. This should cure this habit without a problem.

GLOSSARY

Aviary A birdcage which is divided into two parts, the flight and the shelter. The flight is the outer section, made of a wooden frame and wire meshing, where the budgies fly around. The shelter, the indoor part which looks like a garden shed, provides a place of warmth and protection in colder weather.

Budgerigar Belonging to the parrot family, the "budgie" is native to Australia. It is the most popular of the parakeets and is therefore often referred to as *"the"* parakeet.

Cere The equivalent to the nose of a budgie; there are nostrils towards the top. The color of the cere determines the sex of the adult budgie.

Cock Another name for a male budgerigar, distinguished by a blue cere.

Cuttlebone Oval-shaped bone to be attached to the bird cage, a major supplier of calcium which is very important to the budgie's diet. It also helps to keep the beak in trim.

Gizzard Located in the stomach, the gizzard grinds the bird's food since budgies have no teeth.

Grit A very important food for the budgie. The grit goes into the gizzard to grind the food once it has reached the stomach.

Hen Another name for the female budgerigar, distinguished by a brown cere.

Millet A green food supplement which is not required but a favorite of budgies.

Parakeet A common name given to budgerigars in the United States, due to the fact that budgies have long tails. In other countries, however, both a short-tailed and a long-tailed bird in the parrot family are referred to as parakeets.

Sour crop The crop is located at the base of the bird's neck. Sour crop occurs when the crop is swollen with air and a white discharge appears on the bird's head.